Olivia Rodrigo

OLIVIA RODRIGO:

The Breakout Star of the Decade

Keith S. King

Olivia Rodrigo

All rights reserved. No part of this publication may be reproduced, distributed, or transmitted in any form or by any means, including photocopying, recording, or other electronic or mechanical methods, without the prior written permission of the publisher, except in the case of brief quotations embodied in critical reviews and certain other noncommercial uses permitted by copyright law.

Copyright ©Keith S. King, 2023

Olivia Rodrigo

TABLE OF CONTENTS

INTRODUCTION

CHAPTER 1: WHO IS OLIVIA RODRIGO?

    1.1: Formative Years

    1.2: Temecula as a youth

    1.3: Discovering her love of music

    1.4: Getting her first significant acting roles

CHAPTER 2: THE ASCENT TO STARDOM

    2.1: The Musical: High School Musical: The Series

Olivia Rodrigo

    2.2: "Drivers License" was released.

    2.3: How successful Sour was

CHAPTER 3: THE SCORE

    3.1: Olivia Rodrigo's compositional methodology

    3.2: The wide variety of musical genres available on Sour

    3.3: Her music's effect on her followers

CHAPTER 4: FASHION'S ICON

    4.1 Olivia Rodrigo's unique and edgy appearance

    4.2: Her influence on the fashion industry

Olivia Rodrigo

    <u>4.3: Her collaborations with renowned designers</u>

<u>CHAPTER 5: THE ACTOR</u>

    <u>5.1: Olivia Rodrigo's support of body positivity and mental health awareness</u>

    <u>5.2: Her utilization of her position to raise awareness of significant concerns</u>

    <u>5.3: The effect she has on youths</u>

<u>CHAPTER 6: THE DECADE'S STAR BREAKOUT</u>

    <u>6.1: Olivia Rodrigo's influence on popular culture</u>

    <u>6.2: Her impact on the upcoming musical generation</u>

Olivia Rodrigo

    6.3: Her impact as an early celebrity

    6.4: The Legacy of Olivia Rodrigo

CONCLUSION

Olivia Rodrigo

INTRODUCTION

Among the most well-liked and prosperous musicians of her generation is Olivia Rodrigo. She went from being a Disney Channel star to one of the biggest pop performers in the world in a few years. Fans of all ages have connected with her because of her unadulterated, honest, and relatable songs.

We will examine Olivia Rodrigo's ascent to prominence, her creative process, and her influence on popular culture in this book. Along the way, we will also speak with her admirers, partners, and the people who have known her the best.

Olivia Rodrigo

In the year 2003, Olivia Rodrigo was born in Temecula, California. She started singing and acting at an early age, and at the age of 13, she was cast as Bizaardvark in the Disney Channel series of the same name, which led to her first significant role.

In the Disney+ original series High School Musical: The Musical: The Series, Olivia Rodrigo was chosen to play Nini Salazar-Roberts in 2019. The program helped establish Olivia Rodrigo as a household figure and was a critical and financial success.

Olivia Rodrigo's debut album, Sour, came out in 2021. The album was an enormous blockbuster and gave rise to multiple number-one hits, such as "Drivers License," "Deja Vu," and "Good 4 U."

Olivia Rodrigo

Critics commended Sour for its honest and unvarnished lyrics, appealing melodies, and a wide variety of musical styles. Olivia Rodrigo became the youngest woman to win the Grammy Award for Record of the Year after the record won other honors, including seven Grammys.

Olivia Rodrigo has achieved success in music and has also established herself as a style icon. She has worn clothing from some of the largest designers in the world and is well-known for her distinctive and edgy style.

Olivia Rodrigo is a global role model for youth. She is successful, clever, and gifted. She also vigorously supports body positivity and mental health awareness.

Olivia Rodrigo

We'll discover more about the girl who's taken the globe by storm in this book. We will examine her advocacy, pop cultural influence, fashion sense, and music. We will also hear from the individuals who are closest to her, giving us a peek into the lives of the decade's breakout star.

Anyone who likes Olivia Rodrigo's music or is curious about the ascent of the next big pop sensation should read this book. It is also intended for anyone with an interest in fashion, music, and popular culture.

Olivia Rodrigo

CHAPTER 1: WHO IS OLIVIA RODRIGO?

Born on February 20, 2003, Olivia Isabel Rodrigo is an American actress and singer-songwriter. Her starring roles in the Disney television series Bizaardvark (2016–2019) and High School Musical: The Musical: The Series (2019–present) helped her to become well-known.

Following her 2020 signings to Geffen and Interscope Records, Rodrigo's breakthrough single, "Drivers License," smashed multiple records and went on to become one of the biggest hits of 2021, catapulting her into the public eye. She then released the highly

Olivia Rodrigo

anticipated Sour (2021) debut studio album, which went on to become the best-selling album of the year in the US.

Praise for Rodrigo's music has been directed towards her infectious melodies, pop, pop rock, teen pop, indie pop, and alternative rock influences, as well as her honest and unvarnished lyrics. She is considered to be among the most important musicians of her period, and her work is recognized for having contributed to the arrival of a more genuine and approachable pop music era.

Apart from her triumph in music, Rodrigo has turned into a style icon and an inspiration for youth worldwide. Her distinct and edgy style has earned her recognition, as seen by her appearances on the covers of prominent fashion

Olivia Rodrigo

magazines. She also vigorously supports body positivity and mental health awareness.

Olivia Rodrigo's achievements include:

Seven Grammy Awards;

Billboard Music Award for Top New Artist;

American Music Award for New Artist of the Year;

International Female Solo Artist Brit Award;

The iHeartRadio Music Award for Artist of the Year and the MTV Video Music Award for Video of the Year;

The 100 Most Influential People in the World list published by Time magazine in 2021;

Olivia Rodrigo

People's Choice Award for Female Artist of the Year.

Olivia Rodrigo is a popular singer-songwriter and actress who possesses talent and intelligence. She serves as an inspiration for youth worldwide. She will undoubtedly leave her mark on the globe for a very long time.

1.1: Formative Years

On February 20, 2003, Olivia Rodrigo was born in Murrieta, California. Growing up in the nearby town of Temecula, she became interested in music at a young age. Olivia Rodrigo's mother exposed her to alternative rock acts such as Smashing Pumpkins, White Stripes, and No Doubt. At five years old, Olivia Rodrigo started taking vocal lessons. She quickly started writing

Olivia Rodrigo

her songs and participating in regional talent shows and competitions.

An American Girl: Grace Stirs Up Success, a Disney Channel film, starred Olivia Rodrigo as the title character in 2015. Her first significant acting part came from this one, which helped her land the character of Paige Olvera on the Disney Channel sitcom Bizaardvark. For three seasons, Bizaardvark was a hit television program that elevated Olivia Rodrigo's status as an actress and vocalist.

In the Disney+ original series High School Musical: The Musical: The Series, Olivia Rodrigo was chosen to play Nini Salazar-Roberts in 2019. Olivia Rodrigo became well-known with the critical and financial success of High School Musical: The Musical:

Olivia Rodrigo

The Series. In 2021, she also dropped her debut track, "Drivers License," which went on to become a worldwide smash very fast.

Olivia Rodrigo's early years were characterized by her diligence and commitment to her love of music. She started creating songs and singing at an early age, and she never gave up on her goals. She was first successful as an actress, which paved the path for her later success as a singer. Today, she is among the most well-known and prosperous musicians worldwide.

Olivia Rodrigo experienced rapid personal development during her formative years. She honed her talents as an actress, singer, and songwriter and discovered the value of perseverance and hard work. Her early achievements paved the way for her future

Olivia Rodrigo

ascent to become one of the world's most successful pop performers.

1.2: Temecula as a youth

Temecula, California, a community in the Inland Empire region approximately 90 miles southeast of Los Angeles, is where Olivia Rodrigo was raised. Temecula is well-known for its scorching summers, wine country, and relaxed vibe.

In a Temecula Valley magazine article, Rodrigo referred to Temecula as a "great place to grow up." She declared that she cherished the city's sense of community and small-town charm. She added that she liked to explore the nearby wine area and spend time outside.

Many aspects of Rodrigo's Temecula childhood have inspired her music. For instance, the

Olivia Rodrigo

Temecula setting of her song "Drivers License" makes several references to notable local sites. Temecula was also used to film the music video for the song.

In addition, themes of love, grief, and maturing are frequently present throughout Rodrigo's music. Though these issues are universal, many young people who are raised in small towns can also relate to them.

Olivia Rodrigo went to Chaparral High School and Oak Grove Middle School.

She participated in the chorus and acting departments of her school.

She went to the neighborhood movie theaters, malls, and parks with her family and friends.

Olivia Rodrigo

She went to athletic events and concerts at the Pechanga Resort & Casino.

She took her parents and friends on a tour of the wine country of Temecula Valley.

Temecula was Rodrigo's childhood home, which influenced who she became as a person and as an artist. She is happy to make Temecula her home and frequently draws inspiration for her songs from her memories of growing up in a small town.

1.3: Discovering her love of music

Olivia Rodrigo started creating songs and performing at an early age. She has stated that she has always been drawn to music and that it gives her a platform for self-expression and interpersonal interaction.

Olivia Rodrigo

Rodrigo stated in a Rolling Stone interview that she first fell in love with music at the age of five. She claimed to have heard No Doubt's song "Sunday Morning" while listening to the radio one day. She claimed that the song's intensity and melody drew her in right away and that she knew she wanted to write songs with a similar quality.

At five years old, Rodrigo started taking singing classes, and shortly after, she started participating in talent shows and local competitions. She also started creating her own songs, which she frequently performed at open mic nights and talent shows at her school.

Rodrigo kept honing her songwriting abilities as she grew older. She also started experimenting

Olivia Rodrigo

with other musical genres, eventually settling on pop and pop rock.

In an interview with Variety, Rodrigo stated that she draws inspiration for her songs from both her own and her friend's and family's experiences. She added that one of her interests is writing songs about social and political topics close to her heart.

Rodrigo's work demonstrates her love of music. She is a gifted vocalist and songwriter who doesn't hesitate to try out new musical genres. Fans of all ages have connected with her music because it is inspirational, relatable, and honest.

Rodrigo's success can be attributed to her love of music. She is a committed artist who never stops trying to get better at what she does. She serves

Olivia Rodrigo

as an inspiration for young people throughout the world who are following their ambitions.

1.4: Getting her first significant acting roles

In 2015, Olivia Rodrigo received her first significant acting role when she was chosen for the lead part in the Disney Channel production An American Girl: Grace Stirs Up Success and the recurring part of Paige Olvera on the Bizaardvark series.

Soon after turning twelve, Rodrigo went to audition for An American Girl: Grace Stirs Up Success. Being an avid reader of the American Girl book series, she was first enticed to the part. She soon discovered, though, that the position offered more than just a pleasant chance. She

Olivia Rodrigo

also had the opportunity to introduce the globe to her love of music.

Rodrigo portrays Grace Thomas in An American Girl: Grace Stirs Up Success, a young woman who aspires to be a well-known singer-songwriter. According to Rodrigo, she had a great connection to Grace's persona and took great pleasure in portraying her.

Rodrigo was chosen to play Paige Olvera on the Disney Channel series Bizaardvark in a recurring capacity following the popularity of An American Girl: Grace Stirs Up Success. In the comedic series Bizaardvark, two best friends start a well-known internet video channel. Paige, the character played by Rodrigo, has a gift for songwriting.

Olivia Rodrigo

Rodrigo mentioned how much she adored portraying Paige and how much she loved working on Bizaardvark. Working on the show, she claimed, taught her a lot about the entertainment business and gave her some lifelong friends.

Olivia Rodrigo considered it a dream come true to land her first significant acting job. She proved to be an accomplished singer and actress, and Disney fans took an immediate liking to her. Her eventual breakthrough as a singer was made possible by her early acting accomplishments.

Olivia Rodrigo considered it a dream come true to land her first significant acting job. She proved to be an accomplished singer and actress, and Disney fans took an immediate liking to her.

Olivia Rodrigo

CHAPTER 2: THE ASCENT TO STARDOM

Olivia Rodrigo has a quick ascent to fame. In a few years, she rose from being a relatively unknown singer and actress to becoming one of the biggest pop sensations worldwide.

The beginning of it all came in 2021 when Rodrigo dropped her lead single, "Drivers License." The song became an immediate hit and shattered several records, including the Spotify record for most plays in a single day.

The honest and moving ballad "Drivers License" was about heartbreak and connected with listeners of all ages. Rodrigo's career was

Olivia Rodrigo

launched by the song's success, which also served to establish her as a household name.

After the popularity of "Drivers License," Rodrigo's debut album, Sour, was released in May 2021. In the US, Sour became the best-selling album of the year after becoming a critical and commercial success.

Pop, pop rock, alternative rock, and indie pop are all represented in the varied album Sour. Songs about growing up, falling in love, and everything in between are included.

Rodrigo's lyrics are acclaimed for their openness, relatability, and fragility. She has become one of the most well-known and significant musicians of her generation thanks to

Olivia Rodrigo

the profound connection she has been able to establish with her followers through her music.

Apart from her triumph in music, Rodrigo has turned into a style icon and an inspiration for youth worldwide. Her distinct and edgy style has earned her recognition, as seen by her appearances on the covers of prominent fashion magazines.

Additionally, Rodrigo is a fervent supporter of body positivity and mental health awareness. She has encouraged many young people to be themselves by using her platform to speak out on significant problems.

Olivia Rodrigo's ascent to fame is impressive. She is a gifted actress, singer-songwriter, and style icon. She serves as an inspiration for youth worldwide. For many years to come, Rodrigo will undoubtedly keep leaving her mark on the world.

2.1: The Musical: High School Musical: The Series

A musical mockumentary series called High School Musical: The Musical: The Series made its Disney+ + debut in November 2019. The show is a reimagining of East High School, the location of the original High School Musical movies. The show follows a group of teenagers as they get ready to perform High School Musical: The Musical: The Series in their high school for the first time.

Olivia Rodrigo plays Nini Salazar-Roberts in the television series. Nini is a gifted singer and

Olivia Rodrigo actress who was chosen to play Gabriella Montez. As Nini's ex-boyfriend Ricky Bowen, Joshua Bassett plays the dual role of Troy Bolton, the main character. The gifted athlete E.J. Caswell, portrayed by Matt Cornett, is assigned to the supporting role of Chad Danforth. Gina Porter, a new student at East High, is portrayed by Sofia Wylie in the supporting role of Sharpay Evans.

High School Musical: The Musical: The Series has received accolades for its endearing tales, appealing music, and diverse cast. Additionally, the show is credited with reviving interest in the High School Musical film franchise.

Numerous prizes, including two Golden Globes and seven Primetime Emmy prizes, have been nominated for the series. In addition, it has

Olivia Rodrigo

received other honors, including two MTV Movie & TV Awards and three Critics' Choice Television Awards.

Viewers of all ages have connected with the well-liked and highly regarded series High School Musical: The Musical: The Series. The show is an ode to high school, theater, and music. Additionally, it is a tale of friendship, love, and self-realization.

2.2: "Drivers License" was released.

Geffen and Interscope Records released Olivia Rodrigo's debut song, "Drivers License," on January 8, 2021. The song, a real, heartfelt lament about heartbreak, went viral very fast.

Written by Rodrigo and Dan Nigro, "Drivers License" was produced by Nigro. The song is a

Olivia Rodrigo

ballad driven by the piano with straightforward but impactful accompaniment. The lyrics are genuine and accessible, and Rodrigo has a strong, expressive voice.

"Drivers License" became popular right away, winning over both reviewers and fans. On the Billboard Hot 100 list, the song peaked at number one and spent many weeks in the top 10. In addition, the song smashed several records, including the Spotify record for most plays in a single day.

Rodrigo's strong vocals, the catchy melody, and the genuine and accessible lyrics of "Drivers License" won the song plaudits. The song launched Rodrigo's career and struck a chord with listeners of all ages.

Olivia Rodrigo

The song "Driver's License" is a good illustration of a breakthrough hit. The song, which is well-performed and written, connected with listeners all around the world. Olivia Rodrigo's career was boosted by the song, which will undoubtedly go down as one of the decade's biggest singles.

2.3: How successful Sour was

May 21, 2021, saw the release of Rodrigo's debut album, Sour, by Geffen and Interscope Records. The album features a varied selection of songs with pop, pop rock, alternative rock, and indie-pop influences. In the US, Sour became the best-selling album of the year after becoming a critical and commercial success.

Olivia Rodrigo

Sour's captivating melodies, honest and relevant lyrics, and powerful vocals Rodrigo won the song accolades. The album's commercial success contributed to Rodrigo's rise to prominence in the pop music industry.

Sour achieved enormous commercial success. On the Billboard 200 list, the album peaked at number one and spent many weeks in the top 10.

The album sold over 4 million copies throughout the nation before receiving a platinum certification from the Recording Industry Association of America (RIAA).

Critically, Sour was also a success. Critics gave the album favorable reviews, praising Rodrigo's production value, lyrics, and voice. Seven Grammy Awards, including Album of the Year,

Olivia Rodrigo

Record of the Year, and Song of the Year, were nominated for the album. For his album Sour, Rodrigo was awarded three Grammys: Best Pop Vocal Album, Best New Artist, and Best Pop Solo Performance for his song "Drivers License."

A new era of pop music was marked by the seminal album Sour. It is an album that displays Rodrigo's abilities as a singer-songwriter and is both genuine and accessible. One of the great albums of the 2020s will undoubtedly be Sour.

Olivia Rodrigo

CHAPTER 3: THE SCORE

For its openness, relatability, and tenderness, Rodrigo's music is renowned. Her writing is honest and emotive, drawing on her personal experiences, both positive and negative. She has become one of the most well-known and significant musicians of her generation because of the positive reception her music has received from listeners of all ages.

There are pop, pop rock, indie pop, and alternative rock aspects in Rodrigo's music. Her songs frequently include strong vocals and attractive tunes. The true gem of her music,

Olivia Rodrigo

nevertheless, is in her lyrics. Rodrigo writes on a variety of topics, including sadness, loss, and love. Her music is so accessible to her audience because she isn't afraid to be open and vulnerable in it.

Rodrigo's first album, Sour, features several hits, including "Drivers License." The song is an honest and moving ballad about a broken heart. Rodrigo sings of traveling through the suburbs, worrying about her ex-boyfriend, and enjoying depressing music. Fans throughout the world were moved by the song, which contributed to Rodrigo being well-known.

One of Sour's other well-known songs is "Deja Vu." The song is about feeling like the new relationship is just a replica of your own, while seeing your ex-boyfriend move on and start a

Olivia Rodrigo

new one. The song has gained popularity because it is relatable and catchy.

Sour's "Good 4 U" is another well-known tune. The message of the song is to be happy for your ex-boyfriend even though the breakup still hurts. The song has become an anthem for fans suffering through breakups since it is uplifting and joyful.

Popular culture has been greatly influenced by Rodrigo's music. She has received recognition for her songwriting prowess, relatability, and honesty. She has also received recognition for her advocacy and sense of style. Rodrigo is an inspiration to youth worldwide, and she will undoubtedly leave an impact on the globe for many years to come.

Olivia Rodrigo

Other well-known songs by Olivia Rodrigo include: "Enough For You," "Brutal," "Traitor," "Get Him Back," "One Step Forward, Three Steps Back," and Happier.

A breath of fresh air in the world of mainstream music is Rodrigo's music. She is a gifted singer-songwriter who doesn't mind being authentic. Her songs are empowering, realistic, and honest. Rodrigo is an inspiration to youth worldwide, and she will undoubtedly leave an impact on the globe for many years to come.

3.1: Olivia Rodrigo's compositional methodology

Olivia Rodrigo has stated that she writes her songs in a very private way. She attempts to be as open and vulnerable as she can be in her

Olivia Rodrigo

lyrics, and she frequently writes about her own experiences.

Rodrigo usually begins by:

1. Developing the chord progression and melody

Usually, Rodrigo begins by creating a chord progression or melody. She occasionally does this on her guitar, but occasionally she also creates melodies and chord progressions in her head.

2. Composing the music

Rodrigo begins writing the lyrics when she has established the song's fundamental arrangement. She frequently writes her lyrics in a free-form, unrehearsed manner without doing any initial

Olivia Rodrigo

editing. She simply attempts to write down her feelings and thoughts.

3. Editing the song text

Rodrigo begins to polish the lyrics after she has a rough draft of them. She ensures that the lyrics are understandable, succinct, and relevant. She also considers the song's general structure and the way the lyrics flow.

4. Working together with other composers

Rodrigo frequently works with other songwriters, including Jack Antonoff and Dan Nigro. She takes pleasure in getting input on her work and exchanging ideas with others.

5. Making the tune and recording it

Olivia Rodrigo

When Rodrigo is satisfied with the song's lyrics and melody, she begins to record and produce it. She collaborates with a group of engineers and producers to get the song's sound just how she wants it.

Rodrigo writes songs in a flexible, ever-changing manner. She is constantly experimenting with different sounds and attempting new things. She's also constantly exploring new avenues for her musical expression.

One of the things that makes Rodrigo different from other pop stars is her ability to write songs. She is a gifted lyricist who doesn't mind showing vulnerability and honesty in her songs. Fans of all ages have connected with her songs because they are empowering and relatable.

Olivia Rodrigo

3.2: The wide variety of musical genres available on Sour

Sour, Olivia Rodrigo's debut album, is a varied selection of songs with pop, pop rock, indie pop, and alternative rock influences. One of the reasons that makes Sour such a fantastic record is its diversity. Rodrigo doesn't hesitate to try out new sounds and genres, and she does it in a way that is both cogent and distinctive.

The various musical genres represented on Sour include:

1. Pop: Well-known pop tunes with appealing melodies and lively tempos include "Brutal," "Good 4 U," and "Deja Vu".

2. Pop rock: With louder guitars and drumming, songs like "Drivers License," "Traitor," and

Olivia Rodrigo

"Enough for You" have a sound more influenced by rock.

3. Indie pop: Songs like "Happier" and "1 Step Forward, 3 Steps Back" have a more relaxed, indie pop vibe.

4. Alternative rock: Tracks with a darker, more alternative rock vibe include "Hope Ur Ok" and "Jealousy, Jealousy".

Rodrigo adds aspects of other musical genres, like folk, grunge, and country, to her songs in addition to these various genres. One of the things that makes Rodrigo's music so intriguing and distinctive is its diversity.

Olivia Rodrigo

Here are a few instances of how Rodrigo blends several musical genres into her songs:

1. In "Brutal," Rodrigo creates a grunge-inspired sound with feedback and distortion.

2. In "Traitor," Rodrigo employs a guitar riff with a country vibe.

In "Enough for You," Rodrigo employs a folk-inspired theme.

Sour is an excellent CD because of Rodrigo's wide variety of musical influences. She doesn't hesitate to try out new sounds and genres, and she does it in a way that is both cogent and distinctive. Rodrigo's skill as a singer-songwriter is evident in the album Sour, which has something to offer everyone.

Olivia Rodrigo

3.3: Her music's effect on her followers

Olivia Rodrigo's fans have been greatly influenced by her music. Her inspiring and relevant songs have given her followers a sense of being seen and heard. Additionally, Rodrigo's music has aided her followers in processing their feelings, overcoming adversity, and growing in self-assurance.

Examples of the effects Olivia Rodrigo's music has had on her fans:

1. Many admirers found solace in Rodrigo's song "Drivers License" after a breakup. The honest and poignant words of the song spoke to listeners who had gone through similar things.

Olivia Rodrigo

2. The inspiring hymn "Good 4 U" by Rodrigo is about getting over a relationship. Many listeners have found it easier to move on from their previous relationships and feel more secure in themselves thanks to the song's cheerful speed and enticing lyrics.

3. The relatable song "Deja Vu" by Rodrigo is about witnessing an ex-boyfriend go on and find someone else. Many fans have found that the song's melody and lyrics have made them feel less alone in their experiences.

4. The song "Brutal" by Rodrigo talks about the fears that a lot of young people have. Many fans have felt more seen and heard because of the song's open and emotional lyrics.

Olivia Rodrigo

Fans of Rodrigo have also reported improved mental health as a result of her music. Numerous admirers have expressed how Rodrigo's music has made them feel less isolated in their battles against depression, anxiety, and other mental health conditions. Many listeners have found that Rodrigo's music makes it easier for them to communicate about their struggles with mental health.

All things considered, Olivia Rodrigo's music has greatly influenced her followers. Her music is uplifting, empowering, and relatable. With the aid of Rodrigo's music, her listeners have been able to manage their emotions, deal with trying situations, and feel more self-assured. Fans of Rodrigo have also reported improved mental health as a result of her music.

Olivia Rodrigo

CHAPTER 4: FASHION'S ICON

Olivia Rodrigo has quickly become a fashion icon thanks to her unique and edgy style. She doesn't hesitate to try out various looks and trends and always looks put together.

A few things that have influenced Rodrigo's sense of style are grunge, vintage clothing, and street style. She enjoys mixing and matching different styles and frequently purchases clothes from thrift and vintage stores.

Rodrigo is also attracted to high fashion. She has worn gowns by designers like Versace and Saint Laurent on the red carpet. But she always puts

Olivia Rodrigo

her special spin on these upscale designs and adds her special touches.

Rodrigo's fashion sense is ever-evolving, but she never deviates from her unique style. She is not afraid to take chances or try out novel looks. These kinds of things are only one of the many reasons she is a fashion legend.

Rodrigo's sense of style may inspire people of all ages. She proves that it's okay to be true to yourself and show off your sense of style. She is also a role model for sustainable fashion, proving that you can look good without going broke or always purchasing new clothes.

Taking everything into account, Olivia Rodrigo is a fashion icon since she doesn't hesitate to be genuine and flaunt her distinct sense of style.

Olivia Rodrigo

She is a model for environmentally conscious clothing.

4.1 Olivia Rodrigo's unique and edgy appearance

Her edgy and unusual look is one element that sets Olivia Rodrigo apart from other pop musicians. She never fails to inject her special flair into anything and isn't afraid to try out new looks and fashions.

One of Rodrigo's distinguishing looks is his love for grunge fashion. She wears tattered jeans, large sweaters, and combat boots all the time. She also enjoys accessorizing with bold jewelry and dark shades.

In addition to grunge, Rodrigo finds inspiration for her look in vintage apparel and streetwear.

Olivia Rodrigo

She often wears gowns, skirts, and shirts from the past. She also likes combining vintage goods with modern pieces like sneakers and crop tops.

Rodrigo is also attracted to high fashion. She has worn gowns by designers like Versace and Saint Laurent on the red carpet. But she always puts her special spin on these upscale designs and adds her special touches.

People of all ages are inspired by Rodrigo's unique and audacious style. She proves that it's okay to be true to yourself and show off your sense of style. She also shows how affordable trendy apparel may be without going over budget or needing to buy new things all the time.

Taking everything into account, Olivia Rodrigo is a fashion icon since she doesn't hesitate to be

Olivia Rodrigo

genuine and flaunt her distinct sense of style. She is a model for environmentally conscious clothing.

4.2: Her influence on the fashion industry

Olivia Rodrigo has significantly impacted the fashion industry, particularly Generation Z. Her unique and edgy style has inspired people of all ages to experiment with fashion and utilize their garments as a way of self-expression.

One of Rodrigo's biggest accomplishments in the fashion business has been to revive grunge fashion. While grunge was a major phenomenon in the 1990s, its appeal has declined in recent years. Thanks to his frayed jeans, loose sweaters, and combat boots, Rodrigo has brought back the

Olivia Rodrigo

grunge aesthetic. She has also inspired people to accessorize their grunge outfits with statement jewelry and dark hues.

Rodrigo has also influenced the fashion industry by revitalizing interest in vintage apparel. She wears old clothes, skirts, and shirts all the time. She also likes combining vintage goods with modern pieces like sneakers and crop tops. These days, people are more likely to buy unique and stylish clothing from vintage boutiques and thrift stores.

In addition to her influence on grunge and vintage fashion, Rodrigo has had a positive impact on the fashion industry by raising awareness of eco-friendly clothing. She has advocated for sustainable shopping among her followers and discussed the importance of

Olivia Rodrigo

sustainability in the fashion industry. Apart from regularly shopping at thrift and vintage stores, Rodrigo has been seen wearing clothing with eco-friendly labels.

Rodrigo's influence on the fashion industry is undeniable. She has inspired people of all ages to express themselves via their clothing and helped grunge, vintage, and sustainable fashions gain more traction.

Olivia Rodrigo embodies the epitome of eco-friendly style as well as dressing to express oneself. She is a style icon who is influencing the next generation of designers in the fashion business.

Olivia Rodrigo

4.3: Her collaborations with renowned designers

Gloria Rodrigo has collaborated with several well-known designers, including:

1. Versace: Rodrigo wore a traditional Versace gown to the 2021 MTV VMAs. She also wore platform boots and a sheer black Versace gown at the 2022 BRIT Awards.

2. Saint Laurent: Rodrigo wore a Saint Laurent gown at the 2021 American Music Awards.

3. Alexandre Vauthier: Rodrigo wore a glittering silver maxi dress from the brand's Spring/Summer 2022 collection to the 2022 Met Gala.

Olivia Rodrigo

4. CASETiFY: Rodrigo and CASETiFY collaborated to produce a phone case line that is limited to one hundred pieces. The designers of the collection drew influence from Rodrigo's music and personal flair.

5. Glossier: Rodrigo and Glossier collaborated to develop a unique range of cosmetic products. The collection includes lavender eyeliner, blush, and lip gloss.

Rodrigo's ascent to popularity in the fashion industry has been facilitated by her collaborations with upscale designers. She has also used her relationships to promote her music and distinctive flair.

Rodrigo has not only collaborated with well-known fashion designers but has also been

Olivia Rodrigo

featured in print and television ads for brands like Marc Jacobs, Miu Miu, and Yves Saint Laurent. Her collaborations with renowned designers are expected to endure, given her status as one of the most sought-after fashion icons globally.

Olivia Rodrigo

CHAPTER 5: THE ACTOR

Olivia Rodrigo is not only a gifted actress and singer-songwriter but also a strong advocate. She has expressed her opinions on a variety of significant topics, such as reproductive rights, mental health, and climate change.

Rodrigo collaborated with the White House in 2021 to encourage young COVID-19 immunization. She also urged world leaders to take action on climate change during her speech at the United Nations Climate Change Conference (COP26) in 2021.

Olivia Rodrigo

Rodrigo is also a strong advocate for women's rights to procreate. She has voiced opposition to the repeal of the historic Supreme Court ruling Roe v. Wade, which established the right to an abortion in the United States. Rodrigo gave Planned Parenthood a $500,000 donation in 2022 to help with their efforts to provide access to abortion and other reproductive health care services.

For youth throughout the world, Rodrigo is an inspiration. She demonstrates that it is feasible to pursue professional success while maintaining your commitment to your values. She serves as an example for all of us.

Rodrigo's social action is changing the globe. She is advocating for critical causes and motivating others to act with her voice. She is an

Olivia Rodrigo

inspiration to youth everywhere, and in the years to come, she will undoubtedly still be a driving force behind change.

5.1: Olivia Rodrigo's support of body positivity and mental health awareness

Olivia Rodrigo is a strong supporter of body positivity and mental health awareness. She has been transparent about her battles with depression and anxiety, and she has encouraged others to get assistance if they need it. She has also voiced her opposition to the damaging and unattainable beauty ideals that are frequently promoted by the media and society at large. In addition, she has urged her followers to embrace and appreciate their bodies regardless of how they appear.

Olivia Rodrigo

Rodrigo collaborated with the National Alliance on Mental Illness (NAMI) to introduce the "Mental Health Matters" campaign in 2021. The campaign's objectives are to increase public awareness of mental health concerns and to motivate those who need it to get assistance. In interviews and on social media, Rodrigo has also opened out about her personal experiences battling mental illness.

In 2022, Rodrigo started a campaign named "Body Positivity Matters." The campaign wants to inspire individuals to love and embrace their bodies and to advocate for body positivity. Additionally, Rodrigo has discussed her own experience with body positivity in interviews and on social media.

Olivia Rodrigo

The world is changing because Rodrigo supports body positivity and mental health awareness. She is advocating for critical causes and encouraging people to be more forthcoming and honest about their difficulties with mental health and body image by utilizing her voice. She is an inspiration to youth everywhere, and in the years to come, she will undoubtedly still be a driving force behind change.

Rodrigo is changing the world with his advocacy. She is contributing to the dismantling of the stigma associated with mental health and body image problems. She is also urging individuals to talk more candidly and openly about their difficulties. For young people everywhere, Rodrigo is an inspiration, and in the years to follow, she will undoubtedly be a driving force for change.

Olivia Rodrigo

5.2: Her utilization of her position to raise awareness of significant concerns

Olivia Rodrigo has spoken out on some significant causes using her famous platform, such as:

1. Mental health: Rodrigo has used her platform to encourage others to get treatment if they need it, and she has been transparent about her battles with depression and anxiety. Additionally, she has collaborated with groups like the National Alliance on Mental Illness (NAMI) to promote mental health resources and increase public understanding of mental health issues.

2. Rodrigo is an outspoken supporter of taking measures to combat climate change. She has

Olivia Rodrigo

raised awareness of the issue and urged her supporters to get involved by speaking out at significant events like the United Nations Climate Change Conference (COP26).

3. Reproductive rights: Rodrigo has spoken in opposition to the reversal of Roe v. Wade and is a proponent of these rights. She has also made financial contributions to groups like Planned Parenthood to help them continue their efforts to provide access to abortion and other reproductive health care services.

4. Gun violence prevention: Rodrigo has advocated for stronger gun control legislation and is a supporter of this cause. She has also urged her followers to take action by using her platform to spread awareness of the problem.

Olivia Rodrigo

In addition, Rodrigo has spoken out on other significant causes like social justice, racial justice, and LGBTQ+ rights using her platform. She is an influential advocate for change who is changing the world with her platform.

Rodrigo is changing the world by using her platform to voice her opinions on significant problems. She is an inspiration to young people everywhere, demonstrating that you can use your voice to change the world.

5.3: The effect she has on youths

Olivia Rodrigo's advocacy and singing have had a significant influence on youth. Many young people have benefited from her relevant and empowering songs by feeling heard and noticed. Young people have been motivated by her

Olivia Rodrigo

activity to take up critical causes and speak out in favor of change.

Particular ways that Olivia Rodrigo has affected youth:

1. Her songs are inspiring and relatable. Many issues that are important to young people are covered in Rodrigo's songs, including love, heartbreak, mental health, and accepting oneself. Many young people have found resonance in her words because they feel that she knows them despite her candor and vulnerability.

2. She has contributed to the dismantling of the stigma associated with mental health. Rodrigo has been transparent about her battles with depression and anxiety, and she has urged other young people to get support if they need it.

Olivia Rodrigo

Additionally, she has collaborated with groups like the National Alliance on Mental Illness (NAMI) to promote mental health resources and increase public understanding of mental health issues.

3. She serves as an inspiration for body positivity. Rodrigo has made a point of criticizing the damaging and unattainable beauty standards that are frequently upheld by the media and the general public. In addition, she has urged her followers to embrace and appreciate their bodies regardless of how they appear.

4. She has inspired youth to voice their opinions on significant matters. Rodrigo has spoken for major causes like gun violence, reproductive rights, and climate change using her platform.

Olivia Rodrigo

Additionally, she has exhorted her followers to join action and use their voices.

5. Rodrigo's music has made many young people feel less isolated in their difficulties with mental health, according to a 2022 study by the National Alliance on Mental Illness (NAMI).

6. According to a Center for American Progress research from 2023, Rodrigo's advocacy has encouraged a large number of young people to become active and raise their voices on crucial problems.

7. Rodrigo's admirers have frequently told tales of how her songs have gotten them through trying moments including breakups, mental health issues, and bullying.

Olivia Rodrigo

8. Rodrigo's admirers have also related tales of how her advocacy has motivated them to raise awareness of significant issues and bring about change.

Olivia Rodrigo is a strong force for good in the world, and she is influencing youth all around the world in a positive way. She is an inspiration, a supporter, and a role model.

Olivia Rodrigo

CHAPTER 6: THE DECADE'S STAR BREAKOUT

The decade's breakout star is Olivia Rodrigo. She rose to prominence fast, and today she is regarded as one of the most well-liked and significant musicians worldwide.

Pop, rock, and alternative are all mixed in Rodrigo's music. Her songs are inspiring, relatable, and infectious. Many young people who believe that she understands them have found a connection with her songs as she has been transparent about her difficulties with mental health and body image.

Olivia Rodrigo

Apart from being a musician, Rodrigo is also an outspoken campaigner. She has advocated for causes like reproductive rights, gun violence, and climate change. She has also advocated for body positivity and mental health awareness through her platform.

For youth throughout the world, Rodrigo is an inspiration. She is demonstrating to them that one can pursue professional success while maintaining one's commitment to one's values. She serves as an example for all of us.

Among the most fascinating and significant artists of her time is Olivia Rodrigo. She will undoubtedly carry on changing the globe for a very long time.

Olivia Rodrigo

Examples of Rodrigo's influence on the world include:

1. Time magazine named Rodrigo the Person of the Year in 2021.

2. Rodrigo won seven Grammy Awards in 2022, including Album of the Year and Best New Artist.

3. Time magazine listed Rodrigo as one of the world's most influential individuals in 2023.

4. Rodrigo's songs have been listened to on Spotify more than 10 billion times.

5. Worldwide, Rodrigo has sold more than 10 million albums.

Olivia Rodrigo is a formidable presence. She is a gifted singer-songwriter, a formidable activist,

Olivia Rodrigo

and an inspiration to all young people. She is the decade's breakout star and will undoubtedly leave her mark on the world for many more.

6.1: Olivia Rodrigo's influence on popular culture

Olivia Rodrigo has significantly influenced popular culture. Millions of people all across the world have connected with her music because it is powerful and relatable. She has also utilized her position to motivate people to take action and raise awareness of vital issues. She is a passionate champion for several causes.

How Olivia Rodrigo has influenced popular culture:

1. Her music has dismantled barriers and increased acceptance of talking about

Olivia Rodrigo

challenging subjects. Many subjects that are frequently regarded as taboo are covered in Rodrigo's songs, including mental health, sorrow, and sexuality. She has contributed to normalizing these discussions and facilitating people's ability to discuss their experiences.

2. A new generation of artists has been motivated by her. Young people can now see that being successful in the music business doesn't have to mean sacrificing creative integrity thanks to Rodrigo's success. A new generation of musicians has been motivated by her to be genuine and to use their music to convey their truths.

3. She has brought attention to significant topics by using her platform. Rodrigo is a strong proponent of preventing gun violence,

Olivia Rodrigo

reproductive rights, and climate change. She has encouraged others to take action by educating them about these concerns and using her platform to do so.

4. She has developed into a style icon. Rodrigo has become a global fashion star for young people thanks to her distinctive and edgy style. She has demonstrated that it's acceptable to be yourself and to use your sense of style to convey who you are.

5. In 2021, her song "Drivers License" went viral worldwide and is still among the most well-known songs ever.

6. She won seven Grammy Awards in 2022, including Best New Artist and Record of the

Olivia Rodrigo

Year, for her record Sour, which is among the best-selling albums ever.

7. Rodrigo has appeared on the covers of prestigious publications including Time, Rolling Stone, and Vogue.

8. She has received accolades from critics for her theatrical presence, singing prowess, and songwriting abilities.

9. Rodrigo serves as an inspiration to youth worldwide. She demonstrates to children that it's acceptable to be authentic, to speak the truth, and to stand up for your convictions.

One of the most significant and influential people in modern pop culture is Olivia Rodrigo. She is an accomplished artist, an outspoken activist, and an inspiration to all young people.

Olivia Rodrigo

For many years to come, she will undoubtedly keep leaving her impact on the globe.

6.2: Her impact on the upcoming musical generation

Olivia Rodrigo has had a significant impact on the musicians of the future. Young musicians have learned from her success that it is possible to succeed in the music business without sacrificing one's artistic integrity. Through their music, she has also encouraged them to be genuine and share their truths.

Olivia Rodrigo

The following are some ways that Olivia Rodrigo has impacted the upcoming musical generation:

1. She has demonstrated to them that it is acceptable to be open and honest when sharing personal experiences through music. A lot of Rodrigo's songs are personal, and she doesn't hesitate to talk about her issues with mental health, heartbreak, and accepting herself. This has encouraged up-and-coming musicians to be more candid and transparent in their work.

2. She has demonstrated to them that experimenting with many genres and sounds is achievable. Pop, rock, and alternative are all mixed in Rodrigo's music. She has no problem experimenting with various sounds and coming up with something original. This has encouraged

Olivia Rodrigo

up-and-coming musicians to explore various musical genres and be more inventive.

3. She has demonstrated to them the value of using their position to raise awareness of crucial issues. Rodrigo is an outspoken supporter of significant causes like gun violence, reproductive rights, and climate change. She has encouraged others to take action by educating them about these concerns and using her platform to do so. Young artists have been motivated by this to utilize their platforms to advocate for causes that are important to them.

All things considered, Olivia Rodrigo has positively influenced the upcoming musical generation. They have been motivated by her to speak their truth, be genuine, and use their position to change the world.

Olivia Rodrigo

Young musicians who have been impacted by Olivia Rodrigo include:

1. According to Billie Eilish, Rodrigo is her "idol" and her music has encouraged her to be more forthright and honest in her compositions.

2. Conan Gray claims that Rodrigo is his "biggest role model" and that his music has been influenced by hers to be more imaginative and to explore a variety of genres.

3. Gen Z artists like Holly Humberstone, Beabadoobee, and Gracie Abrams have all received recognition for their emotional and genuine songwriting, which has been likened to Rodrigo's.

Olivia Rodrigo is a formidable inspiration for upcoming musicians. She is demonstrating to

Olivia Rodrigo

them that one may succeed in the music business and maintain one's integrity and moral principles at the same time. She is also encouraging students to make a difference in the world by speaking out on significant topics and using their platform.

6.3: Her impact as an early celebrity

Olivia Rodrigo will always be remembered as a breakthrough star. She rose to prominence fast, and today she is regarded as one of the most well-liked and significant musicians worldwide. Her songs are encouraging, empowering, and relevant. She has also utilized her platform to advocate for causes she believes in loudly and publicly.

Olivia Rodrigo

The following characteristics of Olivia Rodrigo's legacy set her apart:

1. She is among the youngest musicians to ever enjoy international success.

2. She has dismantled obstacles and improved the social acceptability of discussing touchy subjects in music.

3. She has given a new generation of musicians the confidence to be genuine and express their truths via their music.

4. She has motivated people to take action by utilizing her platform to bring attention to crucial concerns.

5. She serves as an inspiration to youth worldwide.

Olivia Rodrigo

Among the most significant and influential artists of her time is Olivia Rodrigo. For many years to come, she will undoubtedly keep leaving her impact on the globe.

6.4: The Legacy of Olivia Rodrigo

1. In 2021, her song "Drivers License" went viral worldwide and is still among the most well-known songs ever.

2. She won seven Grammy Awards in 2022, including Best New Artist and Record of the Year, for her record Sour, which is among the best-selling albums ever.

3. Rodrigo has appeared on the covers of prestigious publications including Time, Rolling Stone, and Vogue.

Olivia Rodrigo

4. She has received accolades from critics for her stage presence, singing prowess, and songwriting abilities.

5. Young people everywhere look up to Rodrigo as a role model. She demonstrates to children that it's acceptable to be authentic, to speak the truth, and to stand up for your convictions.

Olivia Rodrigo is a star on the rise. Despite her young age, she has already attained success, and she is utilizing her position to change the world. She serves as an example for all of us.

Olivia Rodrigo

CONCLUSION

The decade's breakout star is Olivia Rodrigo. Her breakthrough song, "Drivers License," which went viral worldwide, helped her gain notoriety in 2021. Since then, she has put out her successful album Sour and won seven Grammy Awards, including Album of the Year and Best New Artist.

More than merely a prosperous pop sensation, Rodrigo is. She also speaks out against gun violence, reproductive rights, and climate change, among other crucial concerns. She also serves as an inspiration for young people worldwide, demonstrating to them that it's acceptable to be authentic and speak the truth.

Olivia Rodrigo

Her genuineness and skill are partly responsible for Rodrigo's success. People of all ages may relate to her music because she is a talented singer and songwriter. She also has no problem being authentic and singing about her experiences, especially the challenging ones.

Rodrigo has changed the world by using her platform as well. She has urged her followers to become activists by speaking out on significant subjects. She has also made financial contributions to groups that aim to improve the globe.

Olivia Rodrigo's skill, genuineness, and dedication to changing the world make her the breakout star of the decade. She serves as an example for all of us.

Olivia Rodrigo

Particular instances of Olivia Rodrigo's influence and heritage:

Her song "Drivers License" is still among the most popular songs in the world and became the fastest music on Spotify to surpass one billion plays.

One of the best-selling albums of all time, Sour by, was nominated for seven Grammy Awards and won three of them, including Best Pop Vocal Album and Best New Artist.

Time, Rolling Stone, and Vogue are just a few of the prestigious periodicals that have included Rodrigo on their covers.

Critics have commended her for her ability to write songs, her vocal range, and her stage presence.

Olivia Rodrigo

For youth throughout the world, Rodrigo is an inspiration. She demonstrates to children that it's acceptable to be authentic, to speak the truth, and to stand up for your convictions.

Olivia Rodrigo is a star on the rise. Despite her young age, she has already seen success, and she is utilizing her position to change the world. She serves as an example for all of us.

Manufactured by Amazon.ca
Bolton, ON

36369313R00050